Beaded
Lampshades

Beaded
Lampshades

BETH BULLUSS

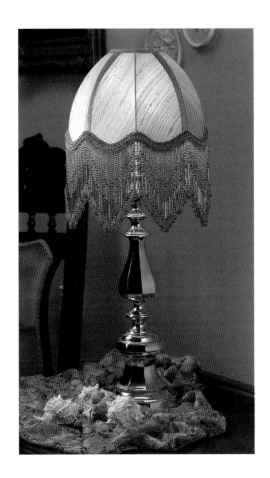

SALLY MILNER PUBLISHING

First published in 2001 by
Sally Milner Publishing Pty Ltd
PO Box 2104
Bowral NSW 2576
AUSTRALIA

Reprinted 2002

Design by Anna Warren, Warren Ventures Pty Ltd
Editing by Lyneve Rappell
Photography by Chris Patterson

Printed in Hong Kong

National Library of Australia Cataloguing-in-Publication data:
Bulluss, Beth
  Beaded lampshades.

ISBN 1 86351 287 X

1. Lampshades. 2. Beadwork - Patterns. I. Title.
(Series : Milner craft series).

    745.5932

Disclaimer
The information in this instruction book is presented in good faith.
However, no warranty is given, nor results guaranteed, nor is freedom
from any patent to be inferred. Since we have no control over the use of
information contained in this book, the publisher and the author
disclaim liability for untoward results.

Photograph on title page: The Old Rose lampshade
Photograph opposite: Cream raw silk with scalloped lace border
Photograph opposite Contents: Even the bedroom can use an elephant! Soft
blush Dupion silk is combined with pale pink, amethyst, gold and black on a
tiffany shade frame.

To Margot, who loves beautiful things.

Contents

Acknowledgments

The shade coverings in this book were done by Barbara Maloney of Creative Lampshades.

Lamp base modifications and woodturning were done by Dudley Keevers.

Thank you to my family and friends for their support.

Introduction

Fashions come and go, but once you have had a beautiful beaded lamp in your life, no other lamp will ever quite measure up.

Such a lamp was part of my childhood. It was a very small lamp with an orange silk shade. That alone would have made it beautiful, but the edge of the shade had black lace 'eyes' all around the outside, and it was beaded with a most interesting fringe.

In the normal daylight, the black jet bugle beads and black seed beads of the background gave off a wonderful sheen. When lit at night, the lavender, amethyst, purple, yellow and orange beads had a life of their own. The whole design was a series of toadstools set in a field of the tiniest seed bead flowers.

It is often observed that stained glass looks brighter and more beautiful at night. This is how the beaded lamp was for me. Not once did I view it other than with awe and appreciation of the beauty of the beads. If the lamp had just been moved or if it had been bumped, the skirt would swing in the most elegant way as if the whole thing was about to dance away.

On visits home, many years later, I would always locate the lamp, dust it down and simply enjoy having it lit for the evenings. It never failed to give me the utmost pleasure.

After the death of my grandmother, I was given her sewing basket, which contained several short beaded fringes. So the tradition continued, and, many lamps later, I decided to record my method of lamp decoration, so that others may have the same joy in making, owning and decorating with these beautiful lamps.

Let me encourage you to try this very simple craft. After just one tassel you will be eager to proceed to the shelf. Then you will be able to make for yourself the most beautiful shade you have ever owned!

Happy beading!

This small red silk tiffany shade has very old beads from my grandmother's sewing basket. The owner has coloured the modern base with oil paint and given it a rubbed finish. These beads have been re-threaded only once in 100 years. (Courtesy of Rosaleen Morrison.)

Decorative Uses of Beading

Beading has been used as a form of embellishment on decorative and functional items across the ages.

Old designs are reappearing in new forms on garments in eveningwear and costume design. The life and light that beads add to garments gives a level of glamour that no other decorative device can match. Once reserved for royalty, the social elite, the film and theatre world and weddings, beading is now both available and accessible to anyone who desires such a treatment to their garments.

As we have seen in the fashion world, the colours and accessories that appear in that field very soon find themselves translated into home furnishings. The luxury of a touch of beading to a cloth, a tie-back, a pelmet, a lamp and cushions is certainly a popular trend in modern decorating.

The elegant, long, fringed necklaces worn with evening dress are reminiscent of the beads that swung so elegantly on dresses in the 1920s, and on parlour lamps of the Victorian era.

Our grandmothers' milk jug covers are now translated into generous-sized covers for salad bowls, and outdoor tablecloths are weighted down with beaded tassels, bringing both aesthetic and practical qualities to our everyday objects.

Christmas decorations are stitched by lovers of beading, and the lucky recipients have future heirlooms to add to their collections of Christmas ornaments.

Handmade jewellery is appearing on craft stalls across the nation and both children and adults are spending pleasant hours creating individual pieces to be worn with favourite garments.

Beading is definitely back, and it is available to anyone who is interested in celebrating creativity.

Page 12 (detail) and 13: This lamp was purchased with a very simple white beads and clear glass bead fringing. The replacement has been done in lavender, amethyst and gold. Courtesy Margaret Hile.

Left and detail above: Very French, the square shade is in taupe silk shot with purple. Olive, gold, black and amethyst beads form a formal fringe. The beautiful base was extended as part of the manufacturing process and complements the shade shape.

Lamps as Decorations

The value of lamps as decorative devices cannot be underestimated. The ambience engendered by a beautiful lamp can produce a warmth and softness to the most formal of rooms.

Lamps with beaded fringes stand alone as functional and decorative devices. When combined with other collectibles and fresh flowers they can bring a unifying note to a collection of loved pieces. These lamps can be placed in front of a mirror for the reflective quality and added ambience.

Even the addition of shades to a traditional chandelier will add an enormous amount of charm as the glare of the globes is softened and the light diffused differently. The addition of beading in such applications should be in harmony with the crystals on the chandelier. Often, the tiniest of crystal beads applied with the braid, or as a trim on the top of the shade is sufficient.

Many of the really contemporary lamps simply need an appropriate fabric and colour to suit the room. But the shape of an unadorned lamp and the base must be viewed *in situ* to make sure that the balance is correct. Any contrast braid, binding or trim should not exceed ⅝ in (1 ½ cm) or it will become a feature and detract from the general appearance of the lamp.

With the wide variety of globes that are available it is easy to vary the intensity of the light and the colour. The soft tones of peach and pink are the most attractive to complement traditional colour schemes. Soft white seems to fit in anywhere. Small globes,

which sit farther from the silk fabric, are preferable to larger ones.

Standard lamps have a place and they provide a real chance for a decorative feature in a room. Attention must be given to the shape of the shade, as the balance is vital. It is probably a good idea to bring home a few shapes to try in the room. Standard-lamp shades are more expensive because of their size and it is worthwhile making the effort to try out shades, fabrics and colours before any decision is made.

A well-finished lamp will add so much to the mood of a room and will last for many years. Regular 'blow dusting' with a hair drier will keep the lamp dust free. Dust will only leave marks when it gets damp or has been sitting for a considerable time.

Lamp Bases

Once again, this is a very personal area but there is a great deal of scope for choosing interesting bases. Because the length of a fringe changes the proportion of the finished lamp, it is often desirable to extend the base so that the hanging beads do not conceal the shape or features of the base. The stem (or candle) of the base must be taller than the average lamp. Electricians and wood turners will be able to do the extension. As well, it is possible to order in a base direct from a manufacturer with an extension done as part of the construction of the base. This is highly satisfactory and assures that the extension is in harmony with the rest of the materials used. The

Page 16 (detail) and page 17: The smaller version of the larger elephant lamp is another plant stand. The same beads were used as in the large elephant, but patterned differently. A small tiffany shade frame was chosen to match the shade used for the large elephant lamp.

Right: Even the bedroom can use an elephant! Soft blush Dupion silk is combined with pale pink, amethyst, gold and black on a tiffany shade frame.

extra cost is only minimal, but because firms have to satisfy their bigger customers first, you may have a few weeks wait for your order to be processed.

Candlesticks, planter stands, brass, glass, timber and iron bases are readily available and are not very expensive. Second-hand shops and auctions are also very good sources of older lamp bases. A special porcelain ornament can be used as part of the base arrangement. It is not difficult to come up with an original idea. Excellent sources of ideas for decorative lamps can be decorating and antique collectors' magazines.

Above and right: In this lounge there are two differently sized Domonique shades. The same colour beads have been used with slight pattern variation. The height of one of the lamps has been adjusted using a small table. The overall effect is harmonious.

Shade Frames

A wide variety of frames are available on the market.

There are many shade frame styles. These include Tiffany, Bell, Tulip, Square, Domonique, Empire, Rectangular and Oval. Within these groups are variations, which include scallop, inverted scallop, double scallop, diamond, tall and wide.

Unpainted frames need to be painted with a gloss white paint.

Old lampshades are often found at junk shops and garage sales. They are usually very cheap and with a minimum of effort can be stripped, cleaned and re-painted for use. In this way it is possible to source some very old and unusual shade shapes. Occasionally the braids and trims can be washed and re-used. It is possible to find some with damaged beading, and these are worth sorting through to salvage some special beads.

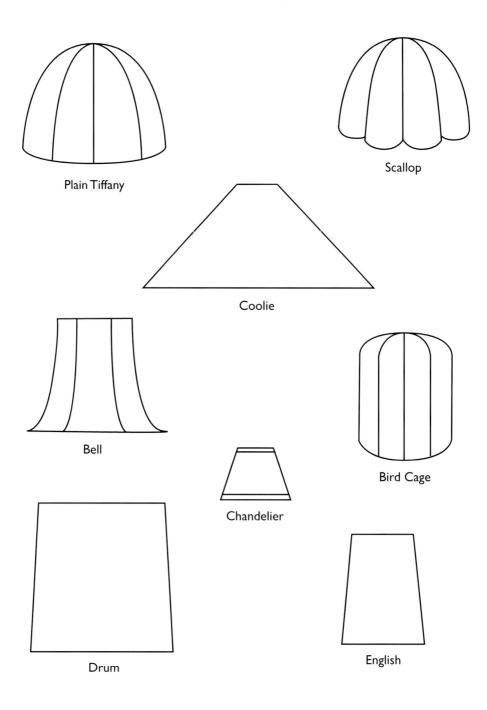

Plain Tiffany

Scallop

Coolie

Bell

Bird Cage

Chandelier

Drum

English

Right: This pretty porcelain base had a white silk bell shade. It is perfect in a pink and white bedroom where it highlights the colours of the leaves and roses in the furnishings.

Page 25: The Charleston is very simple to make. Here, amethyst and gold beads are used on a gold silk tiffany shade. An extra mushroom braid gives the lamp interest when unlit.

Shade Coverings

The shade frames can be covered in a great variety of materials. Silk, satin-backed shantung, lace over cotton, and silk and lace combined are all popular. Synthetics, card and paper are readily available. Check the colours given off by the covering when backlit. Soft colours are best if the lamps are to be placed where people are sitting or dining. Bright or accent colours are wonderful as decorative devices.

The fabrics can be treated with Scotchgard™ if required. A tight covering gives a professional finish and there are many people who specialise in the covering of shades.

Shade frames can have the struts covered with woven cotton tape, ready for a fitted lining and covering. Another method is to glue the outside fabric, then the lining to the painted frame.

The seams of the outer silk covering are best covered. The lampshades in this book use bias strips, of the same fabric, folded in three and then glued into place. Many people use braid or gimp, but these can be a feature in themselves and can detract from the main feature, which is the beading. There are many hobby classes available in lampshade covering.

Globes

Lamps can be lit with a low-wattage globe. The small ones seem to sit farther away from the silk and so make for longer fabric wear.

Cleaning

Keep the lampshade dust free by using a hair-drier. Simply blow any dust from the lamp on a weekly basis.

Beaded Fringes for Lamps

The following points must be considered before adding a beaded fringe to a silk-covered shade: the height of the lamp, the future location of the lamp and the proportions of the finished shade.

As a general rule, it seems that a fringe of approximately two-thirds the height of the covered shade works pleasantly. This would apply to a lamp for an end table or a sideboard. If a lamp is placed high up, the effect of the beading is wasted and the quality of the light is too far away to be fully appreciated. Placing a beaded shade at a lower level can often create a better effect.

Using Ready-Made Fringes

As the beading fashion reaches into the area of interior design, we have seen the addition of ready-made fringing to curtain tie-backs, to pelmets, cushion covers and also to lampshades.

Much of this fringing incorporates the use of plastic beads, and often the thread used is not as strong as the four threads used on lamps in this book. However, there are some very beautiful fringes available and if the design principles are applied, then they can work very well.

The bordello lamp was an exercise in patterning with modern beads and some very old dress bugle beads. The shade is covered in a very pale pink and overlaid with a fine lace. The empire shade complements the formal fringe shape. A pink globe gives added depth to the colour of the silk.

Generally, these purchased fringes are mounted on rayon ribbon and it is vital to use some medium to stop the ends of the ribbon fraying after cutting. It is very important to cut the fringing a little longer than required and then to unravel a few strands of beads. After removing these beads, use the loose thread to stitch off the rest of the beads on the tape. Make sure that the cut tape has been sealed with fray-stop or a dab of glue. Use as required.

Another important detail is to be aware of the fact that the patterning may not exactly fit the circumference of the shade. To cope with this, simply buy the fringing in complete sections of pattern and very gently ease the excess amount of fringing over the whole length of the beading until the pattern matches at the join. Do this with a gathering thread. In this way the beads will still hang evenly.

In the 'Butterflies & Lace' shade purchased fringe and other ready-made pieces have been used in the ornamentation of the shade. Lace panels, lace edging and small butterflies have been dyed in the bronze colours, using potassium permanganate. This is a very beautiful shade, especially when lit.

There are many styles, colours and widths of ready-made beading on the market at the moment and they can be combined with decorative fringing to produce individual lamp treatments. Panels can be alternated with silk fringing and bead fringing. As well, it can be very effective to use fringing and beaded tassels in combination.

This large scalloped tiffany shade is covered in cream silk, purchased fringing, and dyed laces.

Page 30 (detail) and page 31: The blush silk Domonique shade is combined with aqua, pink and iridescent beads to match the wallpaper borders in an all-white bedroom.

Planning a Bead Design

Once you begin to design your own lamp fringes, the possibilities seem endless. Planning a bead design starts with colour choice. The colour of the shade most affects other colour choices. A decision has to be made as to whether the beads will blend or contrast with the actual shade covering. As this is such a highly personal area, there are no hard and fast rules.

Some consideration must be given to the quality of the beads and whether they are colourfast or not.

Be aware that the intensity of colour observed when there is a large quantity of beads is far greater than when the beads are separate, so take this into account when choosing your colour combinations.

A pattern is best designed to include a separating bead, which allows the eye to rest and to separate a group of beads. This can be done with a black seed bead or a dark bead (such as an amethyst seed bead), depending on which one most complements or contrasts with the other beads in the pattern.

To establish a pattern, start at the centre with the longest strand of beads. In this way, the strand can be checked against the lampshade for length, colour and visual appeal. The quantity of beads required can be

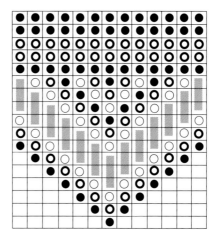

A graph paper design

worked out from one worked panel by simply multiplying the completed panel by the number of panels required.

It is a good idea to allow two or three extra strands at the end of each panel to allow for easing around scallops or just for general unevenness of the panels. If these extra strands are sewn on separate threads of cotton, then one strand can be removed without interfering with the stitching of nearby strands of beads. Unfortunately, the lampshade frames are often not accurately sized and this must be allowed for in the making of the panels. Any excess beading can be gathered into the panel width, with no significant difference to the appearance.

The panels of the lamp can be varied to have one centre strand of beads or three to five central strands of the same length. If a pointed edge is required, then a single central strand is all that will be needed. For a more curved beaded fringe, more central strands are used. Panels can be alternatively long and short for an interesting effect.

Sample patterns can be worked out on graph paper, prior to being tried on cotton.

It is most desirable to begin by making a small beaded tassel, like the Lyndel Tassel. This warm-up project will provide a real feel for the fall of the beads and the look of the finished pattern. Very few beads are required, and you will have a matching tassel to use as part of the decoration of the room.

Beads are irresistible to the touch as well as the eye, but if a bugle bead is folded back against its thread, it can cut the thread. So, if someone feels they just have to touch your beautiful lamp, you can simply direct them to the tassel. A tassel is easily repaired!

This Pagoda (Coolie) shade in purple silk is mounted on a tall black iron base. The beaded tassels on each corner accentuate the shape and provide the only adornment. The dramatic shape lends itself to simple but bold decoration.

Materials and Equipment

Beads

Whilst the classifications are many, the following terms will make it easy to identify the beads used in all of the lamps in this book:

- ☀ Seed beads or rocailles are used as starter, filler and pattern break beads.

- ☀ Small dress beads or small round crystals introduce more colour and texture.

- ☀ Large dress and/or large round crystals are the feature beads.

- ☀ Bugle beads, in various sizes are used as the connecting features. Check that bugle beads are not damaged, as a sharp bead will easily cut through several thicknesses of thread. A nail file is handy for filing off small irregularities, but a shortened or really damaged bead is best discarded.

- ☀ Drop beads, such as teardrop, heart, oval, bird, leaf, magatama and teardrop crystal are used as feature beads at the end of each drop or the centre of a panel.

This Empire shade has been covered in rose patterned damask. A subtle fringe repeating the cream, green, taupe and peach colours adds to, but does not compete with the beautiful roses. (Detail on page 36)

☀ Antique beds of many kinds have been used as well. The quality of the sheen on the small black bugle beads used in the Bordello lamp gave the fringe good daylight display as well. The holes in the old beads are not always evenly sized. This means that the needle and two strands of thread will not always fit through twice.

☀ Pearls—these artificial beads actually have a skin of varnish. These beads need careful handling to avoid breaking this seal.

The bead quantities suggested in the projects are the most economical way of purchasing beads for small projects.

It is important to take great care when using any antique beads, especially bugle beads. These were intended as dress beads where any irregularity of length and size was an advantage. On garments they added extra sparkle and contrast. In a fringe for a lamp, made using the dangle method of construction, irregularly shaped beads will not always hang true and can spoil the whole design. There are examples of these beads used in the book, but they have all been sorted fairly well before being used.

Tape

Woven cotton tape ³⁄₁₆–³⁄₈ in (½-1 cm) wide is fine. Bias
strips of the same material as the shade, folded in half
lengthwise, also work very well. These strips are
particularly useful for inserting the newly knotted
threads between the folds to hide the knots and loose
ends.

Thread

Thread must be strong, but fine enough to pass
through the eye of the beading needle. Nymo
(available from specialist bead stores) is excellent, but
polyester-coated cotton quilting thread is most
satisfactory and more economical. At times it is
desirable to have a coloured thread, to show through
transparent or translucent beads. In this instance, it is
important that the thread is tested for strength, prior
to use. If four thicknesses of thread cannot be broken
by hand, then the thread is sufficiently strong.

Working with a reasonably long thread is very
tempting and certainly possible. The only difficulty
occurs when the thread knots and has to be undone.
This can cause weakness in the thread. As well, if the
thread is unusually long, then the repeated pulling
through the beads will also weaken the thread. It will
not take long to determine your personal preference
for thread length.

Gimp (or braid)

After all of the panels have been completed, they are
stitched or glued onto the shade. Gimp (or braid) is
used to finish off the edge.

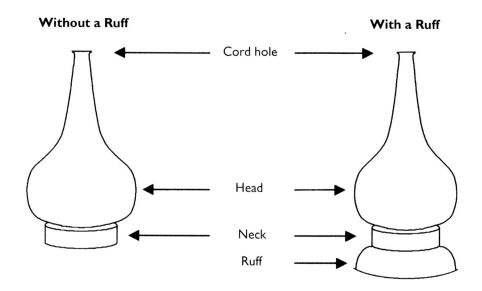

Without a Ruff   **With a Ruff**

Cord hole

Head

Neck

Ruff

Craft Glue

A reliable craft glue can be used to apply the fringe to the shade frame. It is also used to attach the gimp (or braid) over the fringe tape and for sealing the edges of ready-made fringing.

Tassel Tops

These are available from most craft stores. For the purposes in this book two kinds were chosen. Wood turners will make them to specific requirements.

The diameter of the neck determines the number of strands of beads that fit. The closer the bead strands the fuller the tassel. The ruff in particular needs more strands of beads and gives a much fuller tassel.

Purchased or hand twisted cords are both suitable for the tassel tops. Ribbons and rouleau can be used. Fine ribbons can be plaited and wider ones used flat.

Lighting

It is vital that you cause yourself no eyestrain. A halogen desk light with a choice of high and low settings is ideal.

Work-Station

Work at a comfortable height, use an office chair and try to have somewhere to look up into the distance to rest your eyes. Make sure that you stretch your body at half-hour intervals. Long, uninterrupted sessions tend to diminish the pleasure, and you will tend to make mistakes.

A Working Surface

An 8 ½ in (22 cm) turned wooden plate with a small
³⁄₁₆ in (5 mm) lip and an overall depth of ½–¾ in
(10–15 mm), works well as a surface on which to
place your beads. The rough, unglazed surface
prevents the beads rolling around and the height is
perfect for picking up the beads.

A small, framed corkboard can also be a suitable
work surface.

Alternatively, a small dinner plate with a folded
serviette on it will give you good access and prevent
the beads from rolling. A white serviette gives a good
light reflection.

After you have made one panel of a shade, it is vital
that you pin it to the shade to assess its visual appeal.
Attach the shade to a fairly low base for convenience
of work. Then simply raise the base on books to
visualise the finished height. An unsatisfactory
working height will make the stem top inaccessible
and the fitting process arduous.

Bead Quantities

Use small piles of beads and try to keep them
separate for ease of use and to prevent accidentally
picking up the wrong bead. This also makes easy
sorting of the unused beads at the end of the project.
Bulk purchases from major suppliers will reduce the
overall cost of the beads.

*The base of this elephant lamp is a plant stand that has a candle
extension and has been electrified. The finished height is 51 in (130
cm). It is a handsome piece that catches the sunlight in the day and
gives a wonderful soft light at night. The shade fabric is in burgundy
Dupion silk. The beads are burgundy, gold, amethyst and black. A
large scalloped tiffany shade frame has been used.*

Storage of Beads

Glass jars of a size appropriate to the quantities you use will be satisfactory. Make sure that you write the number of the bead, somewhere on the jar.

Waxing the Thread

Some people like to wax their thread for ease of use and to make irregular beads easier to handle. However, none of the lamps or projects in this book has needed waxed thread.

Threading Your Needles

This can be onerous. A good idea is to angle cut the thread, flatten it, and gently ease the point into those tiny eyes. For a big project, simply thread about twelve needles ready and hang them, separated, from a notice board or curtain edge ready for use.

Warning!

Needles often break and they must be disposed of properly. Simply sticky tape them onto a small piece of cardboard and place them in a screw-top jar.

Thimble

A rubber bank note thimble can assist in the picking up of some beads.

Pale blue Dupion silk on a tiffany shade has been made for a girl's bedroom. The beads are blue, gold and black. (Detail on page 45.)

Pliers

Small pliers are useful for cutting out an unwanted bead. They can also be used for pulling the needle through an irregularly small hole. It is worth having two pairs of pliers if you are doing a large amount of beading. Glue some felt to the inside tips of the second pair of pliers. They can then be used to pull the needle through some smaller or irregular shaped beads. The felt protects the needle from scoring.

Bead Doctor

This is a very special tool for threading many fine beads at once. The rotating bowl can be spun fast. At the same time the needle is plunged into the bead filled bowl and the beads quickly rise up the needle. Generally this tool is used when preparing to bead in knitting or crochet work.

File

A small fine file is useful for grinding off any sharp bead edges. The rough side of a nail file is also suitable.

Trouble Shooting

- ☀ If you make a mistake in your pattern, undo it! Do not compromise the satisfaction of a job well done.

- ☀ At times, if the bead hole is irregularly small, you may catch your thread and split it on the return up the strand. Stop, pull the thread back and go in again, using some tension to hold the strands straight. Split threads weaken the strands and you could end up having a break.

☀ When you check a strand, before stitching into the tape, you may find one too many beads. In this case, if it is a rocaille or seed bead, it can be carefully cut out with pliers. Care must be taken to avoid cutting the thread. This should not be attempted with bugle beads or any other large beads.

☀ This form of beading can be stopped and then resumed as time permits, so the project can be extended to fit in with available time. Once you have established your pattern it will be very easy to find where you left off in the sequence.

Getting Started

This book deals with the simplest form of beading. The dangle method of construction uses only a needle, thread, beads and tape. There is no need to outlay on special equipment. The beading patterns are very simple, so the work can be interrupted and then resumed at leisure.

When starting a new craft, or if you have no previous experience in the handling of beads, it is sensible to begin with a small project. You will want to make something that you can really use and enjoy and not just have a sample. A simple and very satisfying project for this purpose would be a tassel.

You will have no trouble finding the right place for a tassel as they serve as delightful decorative trim in many situations. Everyone has a knob or a key somewhere that could be embellished by the addition of a pretty tassel. An alternative use would be to make the tassel in Christmas colours for an elegant addition to a wrapped parcel, or just to use as another decoration for the tree. Try them as bolster trims, on doorknobs, as key tassels, as light or blind pulls, on handles of period furniture, even as sun-catchers in a window area.

All the skills needed to bead the lampshade panels can be attempted in making a tassel. The tassel instructions are the same up to the point of applying the beads to the tassel top. The beads are simply

This cream silk tiffany shade (detail on page 48) would sit well on a standard lamp. Cream, amethyst and gold beads are used with featured tassel drops. (Courtesy of Pauline and Kyle Wilson.)

glued on the tassel top, which is then covered with gimp or braid as required. For the lamps, the panels are carefully pinned on and then glued or stitched on by hand, prior to the gluing on of the covering braid (or gimp) trim.

The beaded tassels in this book have 11 to 22 strands of beading. The shelves vary from 35 to 36 strands, approximately the number needed to make one panel of a lamp. It is possible to trial the pattern for a lampshade and use it for a shelf fringe. Next, you can move to any length, pattern and colour variations for a lampshade panel.

The number of struts on the shade will determine the number of panels required. The photographed versions have been made with either six or eight panels.

By the time one tassel and one shelf have been made, a craftsperson will have gained sufficient experience to handle making a long piece of fringing. This means that in a very short time it is possible to move from a simple tassel to a major project—like a lamp.

Remember that this is a time-consuming craft, but that with each strand the project is nearer to completion. The desire to keep working is sometimes overwhelming. Take time to get your first pattern to your total satisfaction. If one panel does not look wonderful, eight will look no better. This is the creative part of the process so it is vital that time is taken to enjoy making exclusive designs.

The Lyndel Tassel

Materials Required

- ☀ Long beading needle
- ☀ Nymo thread
- ☀ Craft Glue
- ☀ Cotton tape woven, ¼ in (0.6 cm)
- ☀ 11 long bugle beads

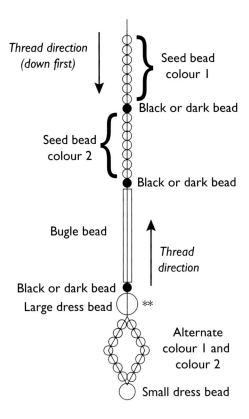

Thread direction (down first)

Seed bead colour I

Black or dark bead

Seed bead colour 2

Black or dark bead

Bugle bead

Thread direction

Black or dark bead

Large dress bead **

Alternate colour I and colour 2

Small dress bead

- 165 seed beads, first colour

- 143 seed beads, second colour

- 33 seed beads, black

- 11 large, feature dress or crystal beads

- 11 small, feature dress or crystal beads

- Woven cotton tape

- Upholstery gimp (or braid) of choice, about 2 ¾ in (7 cm)

- Fine cord of choice, about 10 in (25 cm)

- Tassel top, neck circumference 2 ¼–2 ½ in (6–6.5 cm)

Method

Mark the tape at ³⁄₁₆ in (0.5 cm) spaces, with a soft lead pencil.

Using a double thread about 24 in (60 cm) long, knot the end and stitch the thread into the tape about ¾ in (2 cm) from the end.

Thread the beads using the dangle construction, as per diagram.

Re-thread up through the bead marked **.

Double-stitch into the tape after making sure that the beads are quite straight.

Move to the next dot on the tape and repeat the process to the end.

Glue the fringing to the tassel neck, then glue on the covering braid.

Cut the fine cord to the required length, knot the ends together and thread the loop through the centre of the tassel top.

Making Beaded Shelves

1. Use MDF, ply board or craft board, as they are easy to cut.

2. The edge of the shelf needs to be curved, so, cut a circle to the required size and then bisect it. This will give you two identically sized shelves.

3. Measure the arc, then cut a piece of tape ⅜ in (1 cm) longer than this size. Mark the centre of the tape.

4. Divide the arc into the desired number of sections. If you want three scallops, divide into three parts. For five scallops, divide into five parts, and so on. Make sure that the centre scallop is marked equally on either side of the scallop

5. Decide on the length of your fringe. Trial this on a spare piece of tape and pin it on for visual effect. It is necessary to trial the longest and the shortest strands.

6. Mark the tape into intervals of 3⁄16 in (0.5 cm), evenly from either side of the halfway dot.

7. If you plan to have two strands of the same length at the beginning and end of each complete design, then you will have a margin of error if the fringing is not a perfect fit on completion. You can simply leave one strand off each end without affecting the pattern.

8. If your design is three or four strands too long, rather than re-doing the whole design, consider using a gathering thread to gently ease the excess over the length of beading. This adds extra fullness and will work well.

9. A piece of gimp or fancy braid covers the edge and the shelf is ready to use.

10. Remember, the beads are very decorative in themselves, so choose with care the item to be displayed on the shelf.

This pink shelf is an idea that is suitable to use for a display shelf. The cat in this project had a pink

jewelled collar, so a fringe was designed in pink, black and gold beads. The pattern is the same as for the Lyndel tassel, but the patterning can be worked out so that the central strand of beads is the longest. Then simply work from the centre to the outside. One side of the shelf can be completed by having one or two beads less in the pattern. The other side is worked the same. This is an excellent project for learning the art of patterning with the beads.

The Barbara Beaded Shelf Fringe

Materials Required

- ❂ 1 semicircular piece of ⅝ in (1.5 cm) wide timber or MDF, cut from a circle with a diameter of 5 ½ in (14 cm).

- ❂ 2 photograph hinges (or double-sided velcro tape)

- ❂ Paint to match beads

- ❂ ¼ in (0.6 cm) woven cotton tape, 9 ½ in (24 cm) long

- ❂ 2 oz (50 g) silver seed beads

- ❂ 2 oz (50 g) blue seed beads

- ❂ 2 oz (50 g) blue/green iridescent seed beads

- ❂ 40 silver bugle beads, 1 ¼ in (3 cm) long

- ❂ 42 large pale blue dress beads

- ❂ 78 small blue dress beads

- ❂ 3 feature beads, such as a crystal drops

- ❂ Long beading needle

- ❂ Quilting thread

- ❂ Braid (or gimp) for the edge, 9 ½ in (24 cm) long

- ❂ Craft glue

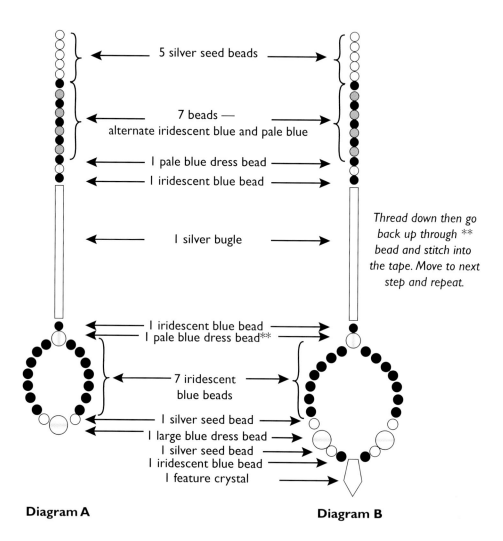

5 silver seed beads

7 beads —
alternate iridescent blue and pale blue

I pale blue dress bead

I iridescent blue bead

I silver bugle

*Thread down then go
back up through **
bead and stitch into
the tape. Move to next
step and repeat.*

I iridescent blue bead
I pale blue dress bead**

7 iridescent
blue beads

I silver seed bead
I large blue dress bead
I silver seed bead
I iridescent blue bead
I feature crystal

Diagram A   **Diagram B**

Method

1. Paint the shelf, then leave it to dry. If you are
   using folk art paint, use a coat of lacquer as a
   finish coat.

2. Attach the photograph hinges (or velcro tape) to
   the straight edge of the semi-circle, 1 ¼ in (3 cm)
   in from each end.

3. Begin at the centre of the tape.

4. Mark ³⁄₁₆ in (0.5 cm) spaces along the length of the
   tape.

5. Sew the first strand as per Diagram A.

6. Create each successive strand and increase the top group of silver beads by one bead each strand, until row eight.

7. Work strand eight as per Diagram B.

8. Continue working and decrease the top group of silver beads by one bead until there are only three beads in the top silver section.

9. Repeat the last strand. Repeat as above from Step 5 for two more scallops.

10. Attach the beaded tape to the shelf edge with craft glue and apply braid (or gimp) to finish.

11. Attach the shelf to a wall using the photograph hinges (or velcro tape).

The Loris Beaded Shelf Fringe

Materials Required

- 1 long beading needle

- Polyester-coated cotton quilting thread

- ¼ in (0.6 cm) woven cotton tape, 9 ½ in (24 cm) long

- A semicircular piece of ⅝ in (1.5 cm) wide timber or MDF, cut from a circle with a diameter of 5 ½ in (14 cm).

- 2 photograph hinges (or double-sided velcro tape)

- Paint to match beads

- Craft glue

- ⅝ in (1.5 cm) braid (or gimp), 9 ½ in (24 cm) long

- 50 g silver seed beads

- 50 g amethyst seed beads

- 50 g amethyst dress beads

- 51 small amethyst crystals

- 130 short amethyst bugle beads

- 7 amethyst teardrop beads or feature pointed crystals

- 60 small glass dress beads

- 60 silver magatama beads

Method

1. Paint and lacquer the shelf. Then leave it to dry.

2. Mark the cotton tape into ³⁄₁₆ in (0.5 cm) spaces, with a soft lead pencil.

3. Use a double thread about 24 in (60 cm) long

4. Knot the end of the thread, then stitch it into the tape about ³⁄₈ in (1 cm) from the end.

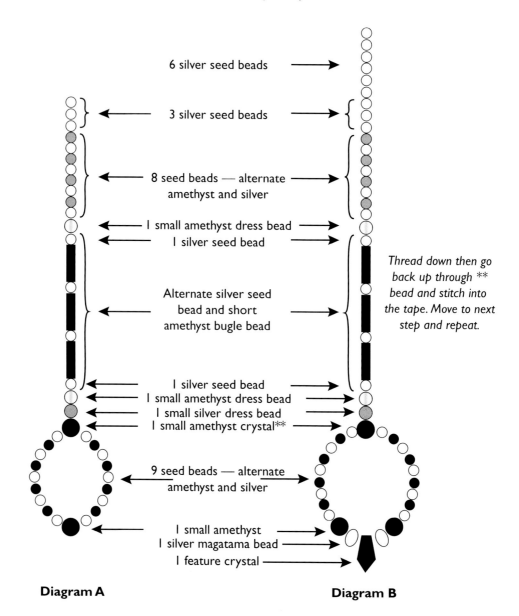

6 silver seed beads

3 silver seed beads

8 seed beads — alternate amethyst and silver

1 small amethyst dress bead
1 silver seed bead

Alternate silver seed bead and short amethyst bugle bead

*Thread down then go back up through ** bead and stitch into the tape. Move to next step and repeat.*

1 silver seed bead
1 small amethyst dress bead
1 small silver dress bead
1 small amethyst crystal**

9 seed beads — alternate amethyst and silver

1 small amethyst
1 silver magatama bead
1 feature crystal

Diagram A   **Diagram B**

5. Follow Diagram A for three strands. See note

6. Then do strand four as in Diagram B.

7. Repeat Diagram A for five strands and Diagram B for one strand. Repeat this pattern to the end of the tape.

8. Glue the finished fringe to the shelf.

9. Glue on the braid (or gimp).

Note: There will be three strands of Diagram A at each end of the shelf.

The pattern change is *only* in the top silver beads section and at the bottom of strand six, which is the central strand of the pattern (Diagram B).

The Rose Lampshade

Materials Required

- ☀ *1 silk covered, scalloped Tiffany shade, 10 in (25 cm). This cover is 'Old Rose' Dupion silk, and took 20 in (50 cm) of fabric.*

- ☀ *Braid (or gimp) to match the shade covering, 47 in (120 cm)*

- ☀ *¾ in (2 cm) wide bias cut silk, ironed in half; or ⅜ in (1 cm) wide, white woven cotton tape*

- ☀ *5 oz (150 g) gold seed beads (g)*

- ☀ *5 oz (150 g) iridescent pink seed bead (p)*

- ☀ *5 oz (150 g) black seed beads (b)*

- ☀ *3 oz (90 g) gold, 1 ¼ in (3 cm) long bugle beads (gb)*

- ☀ *3 strands small olive dress beads (od)*

- ☀ *1 strand (300) olive crystals, medium size (ocr)*

- ☀ *Polyester-coated cotton quilting thread*

- ☀ *3 long beading needles*

- ☀ *Craft glue*

Note: Allowance has been made for 26 strands per scallop. This will seem a little too large, but the sections will be gathered so that excess fullness occurs in the centre of each panel.

Method

1. Starting ¾ in (2 cm) in from the edge, mark the folded bias tape (or cotton tape) into ³⁄₁₆ in (0.5 cm) spaces.

2. Using the dangle method of construction, thread the beads onto the cotton in the following order:

3. 1g, 1p, 1g, 1p, 1g, 1p, 1g, (7 beads) 1b, 1g, 1p, 1g, 1p, 1g, 1p, 1od, 1p, 1g, 1p, 1od, 1p, 1g, 1b, 1od, 1b, 1g, 1od, 1g, 1p, 1g, 1p, 1g, 1p, 1g, 1p, 1g, *ocr*, 1g, 1p, 1g, 1p, 1g, 1p, 1g, 1p, 1g. Rethread up through the ** bead to form the loop.

4. Continue up through the beads until you reach the tape. Make sure the beads are straight and in no way kinked. Check to make sure the strand is correctly threaded, then sew a neat stitch into the tape to secure the strand. Take a step to the next mark on the tape to start the next strand.

5. Continue in this fashion, adding two extra beads to the top each time you make a new strand. This means that the pattern changes in the pink and gold beads only and the rest remains the same.

6. Once you have 33 beads in the top of your pattern (that is, 1g 1p, done alternately) you will have reached the centre of your pattern.

7. Simply work the other side of the pattern in the same way, reducing the number of beads at the top until you have the same seven beads that you started with.

The 'Old Rose' shade ready to trial a pattern. This is a working base only. A taller base used at this stage would be uncomfortable to handle. The first scallop pinned on and viewed for effect

8. Repeat this pattern until you have eight panels.

9. Run a hand gathering thread along the length of your beading tape, and gently gather up the excess, making sure that the part near the top of the scallop does not appear crowded. Pin the fringe onto a panel of the shade and check for visual appeal.

10. Glue the fringe onto the edge of the shade and press it gently into place.

11. Glue the braid (or gimp) over the tape edge to finish.

12. Now, attach the fringed shade to the base, add a soft peach globe, stand back and be amazed at the beautiful thing you have created!

The finished lamp in situ with the base chosen by the owner

The White Satin and Silver Shower Lamp

In the photograph, antique satin bugle beads have been used. However, there are many beautiful iridescent and pearlised bugle beads on the market that would work well.

Other suggested combinations are: gold bugle beads, pink seed beads and pink crystal drops; or dark amethyst bugle beads, silver seed beads and amethyst tear drop crystals. Decide whether you want the beads to blend or contrast and then choose according to your personal colour preference.

Materials Required

- *1 satin covered, scalloped Bell shade, 8 in (20 cm)*
- *4 oz (120 g) short iridescent or pearl bugle beads (irb)*
- *4 oz (120 g) silver seed beads (ss)*
- *8 crystal drops (crd)*
- *160 medium silver dress beads (sdb)*
- *White woven cotton tape, 30 in (76 cm)*
- *Braid (or gimp), 30 in (76 cm)*
- *Quilting thread*
- *Long beading needle*
- *Craft glue*

Method

1. Mark the cotton tape into $\frac{3}{16}$ in (0.5 cm) spaces.

2. Begin with (1ss, 1irb), five times.

3. Add 1sdb*, then 14ss.

4. Thread back through * to form a loop and take the needle all the way to the tape.

5. Check that there is no kinking and that the beads are straight. Stitch the thread into the tape with a double stitch, then move to the next mark.

6. Increase each row by (1ss, 1irb).

Shown here are three very different lamps with similar patterning. The variations are in the bases, the shade shapes, fabrics, bead colours and slight changes in patterning.

7. When you reach the end of the centre drop, add
    (7ss, 1crd*, 7ss). Thread back through * and on to
    the top of the tape.

8. Decrease each row by (1ss, 1irb) until you have
    completed one scallop.

9. Repeat the process to the required number of
    scallops.

10. Pin the fringe to a panel of the shade to check for
    visual appeal.

11. Stitch or glue the fringe to the shade edge.
    Glue on the braid or gimp.

And So, It Is Christmas...

And so, it is Christmas...

Couples who have to downsize to small apartments face many problems, but for one couple in particular, the need to greatly change the kinds of Christmas decorations that they could have in their small apartment was heartbreaking. In their large country home they had always had an oversized tree laden with decorations collected over many generations. Their treasured ornaments were shared among their children and they opted for a small round table decorated with a lamp and a festive cloth. Gifts were hidden under the cloth and assembled around the table.

This lamp was a special commission, intended to make a highly decorative and festive feature in a very small space. And so, a new tradition has begun.

The Christmas lamp is based on a Domonique shade covered in rich gold silk. Gold, silver, red, green and black seed beads have been combined with olive crystals, gold bugles and feature clear crystal drops for the fringe. Natural materials and favourite reindeer ornaments have been used to establish the Christmas theme. A matching cloth repeats the colour and completes the setting.

List of Suppliers ··

Beads and braids
Photios Bros
66 Druitt Street
Sydney NSW 2000
AUSTRALIA
Ph: 61 (2) 9267 1428
Fax:61 (2) 9276 71953

Beads
The Bead Company of Australia
324 Forest Road
Hurstville NSW 2220
AUSTRALIA
Ph: 61 (2) 9850 4923
Fax:61 (2) 9586 2189
Email: beadcompany@ozemail.com.au

Shades, covered, ready to bead
Creative Lampshades
6 Jefferson Street
Adamstown NSW 2289
AUSTRALIA
Ph: 61 (2) 4952 6401
Fax:61 (2) 4952 4200

Fabrics and ready-made fringes
The Bargain Box
Nelson Street
Wallsend NSW 2287
AUSTRALIA
Ph: 61 (2) 4953 8400
Fax:61 (2) 4953 8401

Lamp bases
Brodie Lighthouse (Kaye and Annette)
4/14 Northcott Drive
Kotara NSW 2289
AUSTRALIA
Ph: 61 (2) 4956 1098
Fax:61 (2) 4952 6683

Bead Artistry
Anlaby Designs
51 Swan Street
Morpeth NSW 2321
AUSTRALIA
Ph: 61 (2) 4934 8234
Fax:61 (2) 4934 5326
Email: mariem@ozemail.com.au

Instructional Videos and Commissions for Lamps
Beth Bulluss
22 Gemini Avenue
Elermore Vale NSW 2287
AUSTRALIA
Ph: 61 (2) 4951 6106
Fax: 61 (2) 4955 5491